Bits & Pieces

Thoughts of a Luminary

Ollie "Hoodraised" Woods.

Acknowledgements

I'd like to send a special shout out to the entire poetry community for the support I've received over the Years. Longevity comes with pros & cons. I'm excited that most of my experiences have Been positive. Thank you to my muses you keep me on my toes.

Dedication

As always every aspect of my work is a reflection of my experiences. So I dedicate this collection of thoughts to my family both biological and none.

My tribe (Children) Janequa, Ollie, Jenna, Sedrick, Armond, Armoni, Kendyl...

Every breath I take is used to ensure life is easier for you than it was for me. Each of you have given me a sense of Motivation. My Love for you is without Bounds. Forgive me for my mistakes.

Parents (Ollie & Debra) I only want to make you proud. I'm a work in progress but I hope u see my efforts.

Squad (Team At Ease! 3BM!)

You've supplied support throughout the process. I've studied, Faltered, Gained, Lost, and Learned with you all. That's what Family is all about. #Salute Momentum, Darlin Mikki, Double G, Goddess Warrior, Amy J, AJ Styles, 4 Elevn, Tiger NoTony, Rhema Rhetoric, Kells...

Table of contents

Blame It on The Storm

Aphrodisiac

Soaking in natural moisture

Let it run down the path of my face

I dare not wipe it away

We both welcome more

Splashes

Gushes

Distinctive sounds of wetness

Inspiring others to remove attire

Be Free as Adam and Eve before the tree

Repetitive swishing similar to the breeze of air
through leaves

It comes again

This time so much that it nearly blinds me.

But I need it

Secretly long for it

Because once it peaked it's motivation

Afterwards I only envision

You

I

Bed

Windows slightly cracked

Cuddled

Basking in delight

Encompassed in the breeze

Damn..

Isn't rain sexy....

Blame it on the storm.

Loudness triggers Fear

Fear brings you near

There's only space for opportunity.

Shall we indulge?

Allow inhibition to be washed away?

Let instinct take over.

Nature is in control.

No worries for tomorrow.

Just blame it on the storm

Love by Actions

I finally found it.

Received romance that will leave residuals

Subtle yet lasting energy to show that I matter

She willingly gave

I reluctantly embarked on the journey coined as being "Happy"

Tentatively though

Too many times I've been tormented by a simple loving gesture that masked selfish intent.

Not this time

She took mental Notes

Picked apart our banter to peek at the make up of me

Found my unspoken needs and fulfilled

Heard my unasked for desires then fulfilled

Unmasked pride then drilled in my mind that it's ok to allow her in

I finally received it

That long Perceived fictional character

Invisible cape flaring in the wind

Swooping in to Fix mangled emotions of despair

Salvaging Hope of eventual elation

Super have been her actions

I've finally experienced it

That nearly unachievable feeling of relaxation

Stemming from a needed massage that I never requested

Yet this person is so invested they made it happen

I've finally received appreciation not from words

All action...

Cadence

There's a rhythm your essence screams at me!

Engulfs my movements

I gratefully gyrate to your melody

I dance for you

With you

Because of you

Glances at your strut and I hear drum patterns

A Seductive boom

I'm trying to catch the beat

This cadence is everything

We grind in sequence

All strings attached

Let the winds of harmony guide us..

You're a perfectly orchestrated song...

I'm well schooled in your lyrics

Even offbeat you make me sing beautifully

I call u my symphony

Melanated Male Maneuvers

Mixed with black momma magic creates a catchy hook.

Synchronized with our heart beat

All Heart

Sweet

Never skips

This tango is continuous

Even in your absence

I dance to you, for you, with you

my symphony

Fatherhood

Impact be priceless

Value decreased to nothing more than reasons for negative results

It went left

It's his fault

Dad be demeaned to dysfunction by default.

He be man!

Father

The title that seems to be pushed farther towards the realm of destitute.

That's the truth

Respects aloof

He's designed to carry the burden of hard work and his stress is proof

As He moves mountains

Even after crossing desert plains

"He's suppose to" is how it explained

How dare he expect a "Thank you"

Appreciation be not expected

It would be ridiculous to just give him credit.

He's only responsible for 50% of your existence

Your life's cycle would've been a cycle without his assistance

After mom pushed

He pushed himself to ensure your path be easier to gain altitude

Yet some would rather push him away with attitude

A little gratitude never hurt anyone

The first hero of many sons

Many suns have set with him on the clock

Forklifts loading docks

So you can lift forks from pots

Responsible for meals provided.

The redirection for the misguided

Even when he's collided with the seemingly

immovable wall of despair.

God Like

He's there

Even if stereotypes say different

His back stays swollen to ensure you stay lifted.

Sometimes he's difficult to comprehend cause his love language is encrypted.

The message is simple

His expression is action.

With or without an appreciative

Reaction.

He be Man

He Be Father

He be There....

Up Here

Up here it's just me and my Thoughts....

Cloudy

Unclear

The best part is the clouds are breaking

Revealing the untold

Displaying the unknown.

Invisible ceilings are understood

The blue abyss represents potential

Dare I journey?

I owe it to myself right?

What if I fall?

Is that failure?

Or is the attempt success within itself?

Up here it's just me and my thoughts.

Looking down all I see is people and ants

Nothing to distinguish between the two

I feel gargantuan

Mountainous.

Motivated to be more.

Excel beyond expectation.

Cap less

Fly yet be Cape less

Have a matrix like destiny

To encrypted for the common eye

Titan like

Far from the common guy

Up here I'm everything

Unbound

Free

Profound

Me

I astound

Grounded yet far from the ground

Thoughts take me on flights of fancy

An army of me

Being all that I can be

Up Here away from the madness

Yet in a controlled realm of chaos

Just me

Alone, with my thoughts...

Unsettled Emotions

I'm sitting

This weather is settling,

Mood setting.

As I go over current events I'm hoping these are
things I won't end up regretting

Hope like hell the enjoyment isn't temporary

our chemistry creates temperatures that vary

In a matter of a day or so

It could quickly go

From steamy hot to icy cold.

Colder than a person with no clothes, that got
dumped in 4 ft of snow

You leave my feelings with frost bite

And what's confusing is it usually comes in sequence
of one of those lofty nights

Where the sex was amazing and both of us at least got off twice

Pleasing you is fun for me

So whenever you come to me

I make you cum for me

And it leaves me stunned that whenever you cum it becomes motivation for you to run from me

Humbly...

I'm asking, what's the problem?

Why are you keeping your emotions held back?

King

Reigning over realms is within reach

Extend!

Raise Hands to Handle home

Hone your Honor

Heavy is the Head that Holds crowns

Heroic will is Hefty

Extend!

Healing results from Hard work

Effectively reign

Become Herald of Hope

Recognize Him, Him, & Him can produce Hymns of Harmony

Hallelujah!

Extend!

Reach!

Heirs are Hovering

Witnessing the limited Heights of the Hierarchy

Hide potentially Harmful Hindrances!

Provide upward direction

Be aligned with a divine connection

Effectively reign

Brokenness is beneath your feet

Champion repeatedly repel defeat

The burden of the crown is heavy

Still serenity is within reach

Stress is a burden so release

Wallow in relief

Handle your kingdom

Reach!

I Wanted That Kiss To Matter

I wanted that Kiss to matter

Be meaningful

Lips pressed to lay pause to pressure

Lips lifting life out of limbo

Lips locked to make actual love accessible

Mouthing majestically

Make sacred moments timeless

Pain be a path less traveled

Tongues touching

Twirling counterclockwise representing a rewind back to when the opening on our faces were used only to utter sentences of adoration

4 Lips + 2 Tongues= The great collaboration.

I needed that kiss to matter

Be an astringent

Penetrate to cleanse us below the surface

Grin away the grit and grime just grow

Lips supplying fuel to help us just go

Lip locking be our love language

Passionate kisses be the mortar

Reinforcing the foundation that keeps us cemented in time.

I wanted that kiss to be refined.

I wanted that kiss to remind.

That kisses are how we're defined.

I needed that kiss to matter.

But instead..

You wouldn't kiss me.

She Made Me c Her

She made me see Her

See the C in her

With kisses that taste like concoctions designed for Commitment

Conceptualize Caramel Coated Cantaloupe

Cultivating

Capturing

Contentment in her Core

Creative while Cleansing the Craziness out of Common Cats

I Crave our Connection

In my arms she's Carefully Cradled

Like newborns being Carried

Craftily she Conjurs a spice that's Cajun

Creme de la Creme

Its Captivating how we Combine Cunning Linguistics and Cunnilingus

What a Combination!

Its no Coincidence that Conflict gets cut cause she never Correlates men with Canine

A Conscious mind

As well as the solo cast member in my Concubine

We're sweetly Covered like Candies

Capable of creating an atmosphere as Calming as the seas in the Caribbean.

....I See her

I see the C in her

CLEARLY.

I'll never be Coy about our Cleverly Constructed Contract to Catapult from Contentment to Ceremony.

Crazy Right?

Well being committed requires Courage.

Commotion can Creep into the subconscious and manifest Catastrophe

Ode To Bae

Ode to Bae

I love how you love me just as I am

Never over talks me but you made me understand
that your purpose is to amplify and echo my
sentiments

You stand alone on the grandest of stages

The focus of every eye in the building

Most longing for your touch

Others contemplating

Imagining the jubilation being next you brings

You reject unnecessary static

The goal is comprehensive communication

We never want the message lost in translation as we
transfer energies

You're consistent

Even when I was foolish enough to think I didn't

need you.

My Ego said "I Got this"

Your nature showed me "You had me covered"

I promise to stand with you

Always..

And continue to soak up your power

My dear Bae

Aka...

MY MICROPHONE

You Make It Hard

I want to but ....you make it hard...

I'm trying my best, but you ...you make it hard

I know you need healing and I want to do my part

But my most sincere efforts you always disregard

I'd rather guide you to the light but you seem to want to stay in the dark...

Glorifying your scars

I want to be so into her

No this isn't an attempt to enter her

I just want to love her and count the ways

But now I'm afraid I need to use integers

Cause there's too many negatives that have to be accounted for first

Too many variables that equate to her hurt

And For me that's just no Fair.

Cause me as a positive 1 plus her as a negative 1 still adds up to zero so our connection is going nowhere.

Because of you I understand the pleasure of saying goodbye.

There can still be honor in letting go after a heartfelt try

Lesson learned

Bridges torched & burned

Feelings spurned

Stern is my stance on us finally saying goodbye

Now I'm feeling like even positive memories were a lie

I never knew smiles could be so phony

It's crazy how that I'd rather be happy alone than be with you and be Lonely

If only

You could see yourself

Yet every mirror you own is broken

So you can barely see fragments of actions

Assuming that your outward beauty was final source of attraction

I guess nobody told you that when you have a hideous personality then true beauty is lacking

Are you her

I wonder are you capable

willing and able

Steadfast and dedicated to the task of loving me?

Will u be all that you can be to and for me?

My army of one

My partner in rhyme, crime, and life

The one who I can depend on to go to war with me.

Go to bat for me

All while still openly and honestly critiquing what I write

Are you her?

The one whom I can reveal all of my intimate feelings.

The person I can tell the dirty little details about all my past dealings

If you are her

I have no problem spilling my guts to you as long you promise to view me openly

Because the only way I'll know if it's real when you hold me

 is if you know the whole me

 I'm wondering, are you that woman?

Are you her?

  She that can bring a peaceful slumber to an insomniac

 She that succeeds in areas where others lacked

Comforter

Counselor

Rebel for my cause

She who helps me to recognize and overcome my flaws

Are u her?

Oxymoron

Love be an Oxymoron!

From one perspective we appear to be toxic morons

From the other perspective we're Atop so we pour more on

No care besides the moment

Oblivious to the fact that every negative second pushes forever closer to oblivion

To others it's a bubble of toxins we're living in

We're limiting concepts of consistent chemistry

catapulting closer to catastrophe

But How can that Be?

Cause I easily get caught up in your kisses?

Cause you can't help but slumber to my heartbeat till my shirts filled with your slobber.

Nevermind that the sweet seduction and the serene sleep occurred after destructive disagreements.

Disagreements that are way too frequent.

Clearly we're not toxic!

Right?

Her presence exudes irresistible pheromones
So we must embrace when we're alone.

Passionate sighs

Distinctive moans

Lustful chatter released in distinguished tone

Porn Hub be irrelevant we just use our phones

So disregard that the passion came after venomous tongue lashings.

..but not the kind we like.

But after one of those daily scheduled fights.

When I bellow belligerence that impacts with a fists might.

Or when you slither into cobra mode, hiss, and then strike.

Getting me over pissed like..

"TRICK.. DON'T MAKE ME PUT MY HANDS ON YOU"

Just then your smile leaves me tricked and I'm inspired to put my hands on you.

Cause I know I can handle you.

I gotta hand it to you ...

Woman you make toxicity Feel immaculate.

Not from your lack of love but the way you're lustfully masking it.

Got me scolding the mirror like "Ollie YOU'RE ATTRACTING IT"

"So take some responsibility for this foolery before you start attacking it"

 I'm Done.. ....this is the last of it.

Us.

It's time I do us a favor.

End this toxic behavior.

I'm Out.

You know what BAE text me later!

Temptress

Tease me you temptress

Torment me with tickles from droplets from your tempest

Your temple is a terrific template

Tales of such radiance are only depicted in whimsical imagination

Dashed with a hint of exaggeration

Alas your assets are actual

Fables failed your feminine ferocity be factual.

Your strut speaks a seductive soliloquy

Commanding all witnessing sensory

This sister Be..

Bad!

Badder than mischievous 2 year olds

Truth be told

This Is achieved without the pleasure of her touch

She accepts more respect by not giving too much

Sex appeal is a plus

Some use sexual skill as a crutch

She'd rather fill that mental section than fulfill that sexual lust

Cerebral procreation is orgasmic

Delighted details are more graphic.

There's a star in your presence

Grab at it

Don't half ass it

It's disrespectful to not bow to royalty

Her love and livelihood alone deserves your loyalty

She was the supplement that supplied your initial nourishment

She's that voice in your conscience that whispers encouragement.

She's the Here and now

The where and the how

She be the reason

Consistent

Regardless of season

She's the various embodiment

.....of Woman...

Recipe for Making Love

A lot of buttering up to dull the bitter taste of past hurt.

Full helpings of spice to maintain interest.

An overflow of sweet intentions to keep smiles present.

Unlimited listening so you'll know what's required when things get hot.

Taste often throughout the process.

I'm Hear Through It All

I want to be He

That you no longer lie to

I'm aware that was once part of your survival ritual.

You were forced to fabricate scenarios due to physical abuse being typical

Know that you can escape to me through your truths

My hands will rise only to block blows meant to demean

I mean to protect

First you have to allow it

If there's no enemy amongst us

Then there can be none against us

So decide if us is your final destination

Reassess your reservations

I'm here even when your impulses begin to push.

Your fists can pound my chest like an Alpha male feeling himself.

I'll only feel myself standing stronger in faith.

A knight minus the armor

So nights are more blissful

Let lies lay unspoken until decay

Honor us with honesty

Lighten your burden by laying it on me heavy

I'll hear you

Help heal you

Hold you to higher standard

Until we're standing in agreement

We'll be thick as thieves

Solid as cement

Dissolve your desire to deceive

Drop your guards and believe

Know I'll love you through it all

Ready Set Grow

You keep me centered

Focused

Not for me

My life belongs to you

Back pains are in the fine print of Fatherhoods'
contract

I been signed up

I can't say you'll never see struggle

I'll only promise to block most of it from reaching
you

Even as athletes we're not designed to run away

We stand

We stay

Home is where the heart is

Thankfully we're blessed with plenty

Use that privilege to your benefit

You shall prosper!

We shall continue

Charge towards aspirations

Ready?

Set ?

GROW!

I hope you know thoughts of you make me bubble with pride.

How individually you push hindrances aside.

There's strength in our numbers

Look at us side by side.

Multiple variations of the same flesh

Stomping into manhood is the destination

We're on the same quest

My goal is to clear the path ahead

Minimize your concern

Making the load you carry a lil Lighter

While ensuring you're still Forced to learn

Ready?

Set?

Grow!

The Legacy Wins

You're my reflection

So, I work to remove the cracks in the mirror

You need not see broken

Only parts of your concrete legacy

Your grandfather's blood was mixed with mortar

Strengthening his frame to be unbending

I had the broadest shoulders to stand on

The weight of generations he carried until I was
ready

Now the batons in my hand

But don't hurry

Pace yourself to greatness

Mountain peaks feel higher

When you took time to climb

Be diligent

Short Cuts are for bad barbers.

Embrace the struggle

Resistance motivates endurance

Accomplishment is your purpose

Pride is your insurance.

Son

You're up next!

Take nothing for granted

The foundation's been laid

Seeds been planted

Consistent encouragement as your nourishment

Awareness is your secret weapon

Consider all factions before you maneuver.

Strategy rarely needs second guessing.

Son!

Never look back for yours is covered.

By Fathers,

Grandfathers,

Uncles and Brothers.

See Man..

Be Man

That's the motto.

As you wrestle with life

Be more savage than macho.

Avoid allowing your ego to swell from false bravado

Take heed

Then bravo.

The Legacy Wins...

It's your time

Son.

Subliminal Minds

A place where

the broken truly begin to become whole

Ceilings become invisible

Accomplishing the improbable becomes common ritual

Limitations hindered only by your imagination

Dreams are given detail

Ambition fuels fire

You break through self Imposed restraints Like Latinos to Trump's imaginary wall

You end the game of infinity wars with a single finger snap

You control the gem of time so you can just pause, rewind, and bring it back.

You're titan like.

Hercules with twice the might.

Darkness is nonexistent your voice is light.

She Was There

The most supportive

Loving,

Endearing,

Uplifting,

Thing she said was nothing!

Just stood drenched in raindrops

Arms extended

Eyes filled with concern.

One hand wiping away endless tears

The other cuffed my waist firmly.

An affectionate embrace for my benefit.

No words

Her gaze screamed protection.

She loves me

Hates my hurt

The cause even more so

Silently Just pressed her head to my torso

"Come here allow me to love on you" said her actions

Gently massaged my individual fingers

Not allowing stress to linger

With a subtle stroke of my rain drenched beard I swear I heard "Babe you're enough. You're stronger than all your distractions"

Still her lips never moved

All effort

Golden rule in effect

In times of despair she didn't forget to BE THERE

That's what most men seek

Her lip gloss left a stamp of admiration on my cheek

No need to speak

Just reinforced that my vulnerability is safe

Every moment

Any space

I won't always hear her voice

But I should get accustomed to her face

She'll be there

Lovingly

Endearingly

Saying Nothing...

She's Caramel Coated

She's Caramel Coated

Beauty coded In her DNA

I can no longer keep desire pinned up

During his creative process God's Imagination went nuts

He designed the mold of you then broke it

He wanted radiance and once he spoke it

A Presence manifested and all took notice

What Came forth is the reflection u see daily

Queendom personified

Endearing smile

Astonishing eyes

We all feel blessed by captured glimpses

I've been smitten by your existence.

You Just don't know what your smile does to me

Makes me wanna submit to you lovingly

There's no better thought than you loving me

My caramel Coated Goddess

Granny

I remember vividly coming home from a 10 hour shift to an apartment that was normally hot, but on this evening had an eerie chill to it, a cold silence. The only sound was my mother Debra Woods whispering to my grandmother. Yet as I got closer to the room where Granny usually slept I heard that sound that still gives me chills. A laboring breath that the hospice nurse labeled "The Death Rattle". I remember coming to kiss my mom on the forehead and doing the same to our Matriarch. Raisha Moore stood behind My mom as we talked about family and reminisced about favorite memories. As I was about to exit the room I heard the breathing speed up. I turned and watched as her chest no longer moved in and out from the breathing. One Long Exhale, followed by ONE SINGLE TEAR ROLLED DOWN HER CHEEK. Mom SCREAMED "MOMMA NO .. AS she squeezed her hand. Raisha grabbed mom before she could fall to the floor and they wept together. I ushered them out the room. I kissed Granny and wiped her tears. I swear I saw pain no more. Only peace. I didn't get to weep. I got in "Let me take care of things mode". I reached out to the

Family and said "Its time; get over here". For the next couple hours the family piled into my apartment consoling each other and telling the greatest stories of Grandma. Then the coroner van came. One person. He needed help. So I had to assist in wrapping her Up, carrying her down the stairs, placing her body in the van. The family Stared out all of the windows. Not a word spoken. Countless tears shed. At that moment. I finally broke down. I had the honor of wiping away my granny's last tear... 8 years ago TODAY..

Yea, I Snooped

I felt like we were living an untruth

So I snooped

Peeped the scoop

Recognizing my instincts I needed to listen to

I guess you didn't understand that men have "Intuition" Too

Although normally you're brash and bold

I wasn't fully sold

Plus I knew that you didn't know that I knew your code

 the times we were arguing and fighting

I saw you constantly scrolling, typing, and swiping

So the moment you were sound asleep

The time was found to creep

Glance and peeped

Got confirmation to the assumptions that had me vexed within

How even while on the phone with me you'd be texting him

Stressing me while sexing him

Giving less to me and the best to him

Giving proof that women also make decisions based off rises in their estrogen

Got me questioning my own abilities

I'm sending sweet nothings

But receiving nothing but hostility.

So yeah silly Me..

I snooped.

Violated your privacy

Only to shed light on lies you provided while locking eyes with me

How engulfed you are in the other life u live privately

Glad I pried to See

It hurts to know you know longer take pride in me

Your Hearts been stolen! Emotional Piracy.

But wisely for the wondering eyes I keep a grin

Still feeling the anguish behind seeing Y'all plans for Sweetest Day weekend

You told him I'd be working

And you had a location for him to come receive his GIFT and put work In

It would be a pleasure filled hook up for certain

I'm hurting

but working on my exit plan

Searching for more shallow waters cause I'm in too deep

I'm now looking upward all because I peeped

I've never been so happy to be a creep..

Happy Sweetest to you and him

Fixated on A Façade

I've faced the facade.

Fixed it

Found that some people are just fickle

Fond of phony

Focused on confusion

Trapped in the illusion

That finger pointing makes more sense than being responsible for your own actions

Your maturity is lacking

If you believe that your choices don't play a part in life's choices

Your hardships are just God's voice nudging you to wake up

Start self reflection

And eventually your acceptance of the lessons

For me the common misconception

 is that I spurn love

That's inaccurate I've just been concerned that loves been misrepresented.

I keep hearing it's endearing

Yet I've seen it make life go hard

If its designed strictly for me then why do you have to fight so hard.

It's so hard for the theory to sink through

If what I'm hearing is right and I'm naturally grinchy then that means somewhere is my Cindy Lue

She who'll embrace my differences instead of complain that I'm not what she's accustoms to

She who'll help to smooth out my ruff edges to ensure we fit right.

She who's mature enough to converse with me until we gain understanding when things don't sit right

As of now I'll just sit tight

Like several big bodies in a back seat

I'm looking for a natural rhythm instead of us being

off key always missing the back beat

stressing along lacking relief

Maybe I'm unrealistic

But if love is the truest source of personal power
then accepting me for who I am should be simplistic

I'm attempting to decipher this concept the best way
that I can

Is she selfish for only wanting to love me if I change
or am I selfish for wanting to be loved just the way I
am?

Or is love selfish in general?

How can it be when bonding between 2 people is the
basic principle?

Giving up too much of your natural make up so
someone will Love you seems incomprehensible

Less than sensible

A major factor in SELF Love is staying true to you

So, if the best of me still won't do

I'll see that as my cue

Begin my strut away and...

 I'll wait for my Cindy Lue

I Be Kin

I be Kin

I be Kin then add a G

Cause this King be

 Grasping Goals Godlike or Going Gorilla if my
family needs me.

I be Teflon

Immune to the shots fired, daggers aimed, or cleats
on the feet on my back that people tried to step on.

I be Kin

I mean I be King

I be superior

You be sloppy

I be accomplished yet you be cocky

I be maneuvering while you

Just watch Me

But watch the side-eyes cause I box with the creed of Rocky

I Be champion

I stand strong In life's fist fights

You cant stand in my shoes they don't fit right

I be giant

You want me minimized

I be victorious yet YOU wanna villainize

Same cats needed my help threw shade once they've been obliged

You can't overshadow a giant I'm too close to the Sun that's why I stay energized

I be Monarch

With this Movement I be Melanated Mozart

While you be Tin Man

You move with no heart

Just an empty space in that chest groove

You be pawns unfamiliar with chess rules.

You be sacrificed.

I be gargantuan

You be unworthy of my shadow that you standing in

I be the blueprint

I be the guidelines

but you be the mockery

Even if I gave you the hard copy

It'll be hard for you to copy me

Cause I go farther

I mean I Be Father

I be double shifts to cover bills and daughters special gifts

And sons' trips to the ballpark.

I be the bearer of struggle yet disrespected by hallmark

When I see Happy Father's Day to all the ladies on these cards in Walmart.

I be a presence

I be arms occupied cause I'm baring Presents.

I be Support. Child. Check.

While u just see child support checks

I be the difference maker

Yet to some I be irrelevant

I be the person who falls short

And works even harder for betterment

I be Alpha male

But still understand that I can still salute other kings

I be Leader, teacher, and greatness personified

Amongst other things

I be the triple M

Melanated Male Movement

I be the anchor to a floating champions ship

but this isn't a brag the actions already proved it

I be the shield

My purpose is to protect the next generation of soldiers

I be the Black Hercules carrying entire generations on my shoulders

I be the model of perseverance that won't bend until the struggle is over

I be Kin.

I be Kin then add a G

Cause this King be

 Grasping Goals Godlike or Going Gorilla if my family needs me

I Be Man

More than Male

Too Mature to be Boy

Man!

Accidental Attraction

It was an accidental attraction

Unexpected to happen

Something that manifested thru innocent actions

Pleasant conversation, giggles & laughin

Her against males me against females both of us bashin

Only to find out we have similar passions

She slowly building up my interest with every question she askin

Connection building stronger with every moment that's passin

Were oblivious to what's happening and nobody's even thinking bout askin

Maybe its cause our at home situations are

unfulfilling and were tired of the tantrums and verbal lashings

So somebody providing peace of mind right now is certainly what's happening

Although my mental warning sign is certainly flashin

All I care about is this feeling ...not the trouble that's masked within

Like that spontaneous kiss tongues wagging and lips smackin

Willpower Crashin

Bra unlatched then

Pants unfastened

Bodies becoming one and commence the act of smashin

Bodies moving with a passion back and forth like we battlin

No time for relaxin

We both want that specific reaction

Pound and pound till our bodies pass out from climaxin

When we were done there was no braggin

Jus sat back in the glow baskin

 there were no regrets to our actions.

Jus back to laughin

About our accidental attraction

And how we created a memory that will be everlasting

Along The Way

Along the way you forgot to love me

For years our strut through life was in sequence

The goal was progress if even only an inch at a time

Attached at the hip while facing the grind

Future is stratospheric if fate is aligned

I manufactured serenity in multiple ways in my mind

Then the mirror revealed stress in my face with these lines

Attempting to ignore the fact our nights were less steamy and dates have declined

I wanted negative reasons erased from our rhymes

We traveled the tracks on this relationship train and even had future stations in mind

But was it a treasure or overextended waste of our time?

Cause along the way you forgot to love me

Me!

Not what I could make pleasing to you

It never sunk in that things were hard for me because I wanted it Easy for you.

You forgot to appreciate the ache in my shoulders from carrying your burdens.

You never saw the sacrifice because it was for your benefit

You got to bask in the shine of the sunny of beaches while I struggled to pay for the trip

That's what love does

It pushes the bounds of sanity to allow the perception of a perfect reality

Selflessly

Yet with Reciprocity

So my overworked back asks

"Where's the love?"

Why must I Beg for what should be delivered passionately and naturally?

One would say it's better to Give than receive

That's until they've given until exhaustion

A word of caution

The Mirror is honest

If what you see is less than flattering

Life is no longer similar to what you've been imagining

Then what's missing is love

From others and more importantly self

Actions must support statements

If your energy isn't matched then lack of understanding is blatant

You have to change this

Along the way never forget to love you...

A Pleasant Reminder

I entered the room and was immediately confronted with a bewitching fragrance

Vikki couldn't have kept this secret long

Sweet but strong

100% intoxicant

Mixed strategically with oxygen

The mixture provided instant stimuli

Effervescent seduction bouncing around my nostril

 I almost forgot what that smelled like

Then we hugged for what seemed like forever

Her head planted gently to my chest

Breaths and heartbeat become synchronized

Heads lifted only to lock eyes

Then lips.

Then tongues

Whisked wonderfully into a wet Waltz leaving the results of wanting more

A reassuring passionate embrace.

I almost forgot what that felt like

Romance was the catalyst for a more intense encounter

I needed only what she could provide

I'd thrust

She'd counter

I'd move sensually

She'd instruct me to pound her

Pausing only to kiss

Then switch

As she displayed that modern cowgirls exist.

Slowly there was stride in her hips

We made up lost time

With sheets wet

Earned Sweat

Vigorous intimacy combined with intense sex..

I almost forgot what that felt like.

I appreciate the reminder...

Through Broken Mirrors

Her face radiated innocence

But her eyes displayed an embedded anguish

Maneuvering me upon an emotional seesaw

I stared into her soul's windows and saw what she saw

The eldest of the surviving offspring

They asked if she was aware

Flashback to the night before

Pictures vivid like she was back there

A 7-year old's nightmare

She saw blood stained razor blades accompanied by random splatter

She saw a sink vandalized by pill filled Vomit from a failed overdose.

Then tears evolved into a monsoon drenching her face as she remembered the scene that "Did it"

Graphic!

Explicit!

She noticed her favorite past time

Her jump rope tied in Noose form strategically hanging from the vent

Then she pictured her mother's life source absent

away her mother's life went

Taken by the very object that brought her the most joy

Now A self inflicted weapon no longer a toy

A wail released that brought us all back to reality

She grabbed me as our tears fell gradually

I know now that she witnessed her mother's Suicide Scene.

She.

She was only 7.

The Letter to Love

Greetings love.

Some of my peers have nudged me to write to you.

The real you. Not the over stated yet vastly watered-down version. Love I know you to be grounded in reality. The place where life exists. The love I believe in isn't polished and perfect. When a person's imperfections arise is when real love appears to wipe away the smudges.

Love you're selfless. Every action committed, every gesture performed, and Every word spoken is for the betterment of another. What's being glorified is love based upon condition. "I Love you because of what you do for me or because how you make me feel", Yet that's not genuine.

Love is the man that works tirelessly to provide for his people and decides to wake up on an off day to feed the less fortunate. Glory to the action. I apologize for my love. Some of us poets have lessened your value

By attaching your title to unworthy movements. Lust confused as love appreciation without reciprocity seen as love

Those things are powerful but incomplete. That leaves so many who straddle the fence actually backing off. When you're truly in love it's monumental. So how does that end and you're allegedly feeling it again with someone else two weeks later?

Love it's not that I don't believe in you I just don't honor what I've seen. I refuse to fake like running in slow motion through a deceitful, heartless, concrete jungle is the same as sipping libations, bonding, while relaxing on a bed of rose petals.

Love if you're losing believers you have to blame your Messengers. Fire them for misrepresentation.

I know you to be a continuous commitment to living in a hard to find destination. I know you're way more than a word.

Sincerely

The Grinch

(After he's talked to Cindy Lou and Martha Mae)

¯_(ツ)_/¯

Religious Hypocrisy

I wonder how "the Most High" feels about you
manipulating his word to justify your own theory

Screaming to world that you're a virtuous girl but
your attitude leaves most people leery

We are all aware that the book says to "find a wife is
a good thing"

But it wasn't intended to devalue the presence of a
man making him feel less than a king

You're the Raven Symone of Christianity

So stuck in your own insanity

That you think it's ok to degrade others

Casting stones in your glass house

Turning your nose up while simultaneously
expecting acceptance

How rude

Luckily for you the highest is still working on me

being a different dude

Or your blatant insults would've warranted immediate retaliation

Thick is the skin I'm in so I don't need your validation

I snicker at your "Holier-than-thou " Exaggerations.

Your actions only display a judgmental hypocrite

Honestly your full of crap and your peers are starting to get a whiff of it

We're supposed to be beacons while speaking

teaching non believers to have faith beyond sight

But since you seek to condemn

Your inner glow is dim

To me you're an artificial light..."

I see you Judging me through your tainted eyes

You Disguise your arrogance behind religious beliefs

You justify Turning your nose up as Christian values

Christian...

Christ Like...

How do you think he feels when one of his creations

deems themselves to be better than another?

Is He pleased?

What if I told you that I value my relationship with God and he's still working on me?

Would you still think you're better?

If so, you need a refresher course in humility

But I digress

I'll leave you be

I mean who am I to Judge anyway...

Ponder that. ...

About the Author

Hoodraised has released 6 CD's "Transitions" 2007, "Lion and the Mic" 2009, "Mind over Matters" 2013 which have gotten rave reviews from the "Spoken Word Lounge Magazine" and blogs Such as "Mr. Openyenated", Refocused 2014, Invisible Ceilings 2015 and in 2017 he released Jotted Gems a book and album that explored his personal journey as a man . He holds several titles as a national award winning poet 2017 NPA's Erotic poet of the year, Open mic of the year, "The Malik Yusef Wordsmith of the year award 2013, Lyricist of the year Prince of Poetry", The Spoken Word Lounge King Pen" and was honored at The Rising Stars Entrepreneurs Gala for being a positive influence in his neighborhood. He has also had several poems published in various newspapers. He's opened up for Grammy Award winning artist Malik Yusef, Mary and has shared the stage with BET, Netflix, and Comedy Central comedians B. Cole, Shawn Morgan and T.Murph. Hood is taking his talent in Spoken Word to a new level, staying true to his words "I don't have to change my space in order to change my fate".

JOTTED
Gems

HOOD RAISED

80

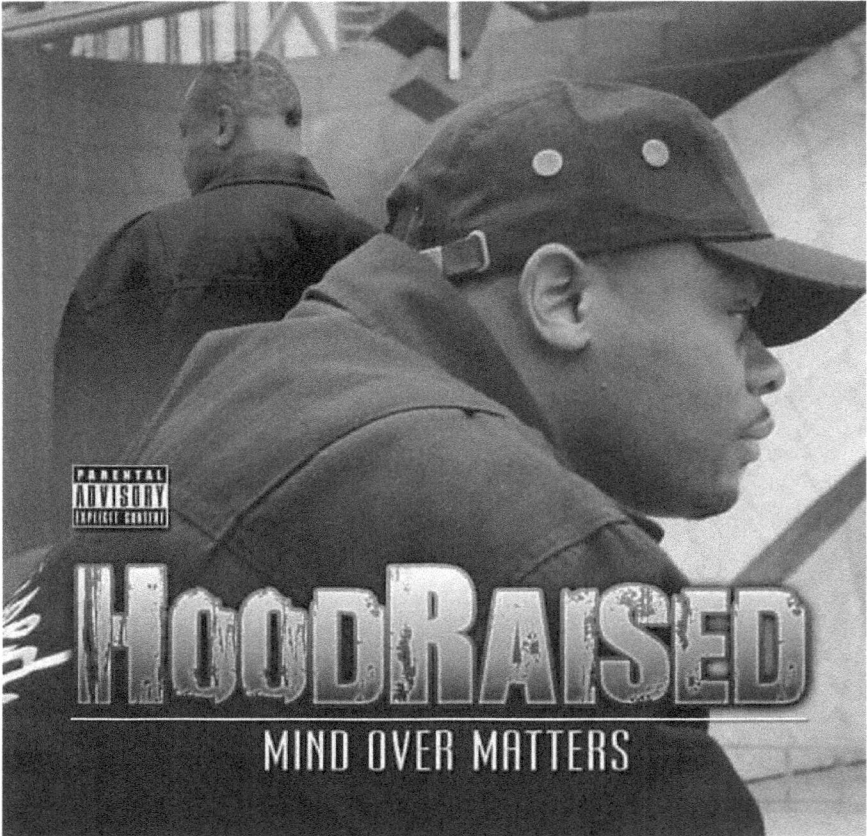

Jotted Gems
Road to a Milestone
THE SOUNDTRACK
HOOD RAISED
312-823-7438
HOODWOODS@GMAIL.COM
HOODRAISED
HOODRAISED1000

HOOD
RAISED
REFOCUSED
#PoetMode
www.artistecard.com/Hoodraised
www.soundcloud.com/Hoodraised
Download the Artist App:Hoodgems